Parents of the Passion

SEVEN LENTEN MONOLOGS AND COMPANION WORSHIP SERVICES

William R. Grimbol

C.S.S. Publishing Co.
Lima, Ohio

PARENTS OF THE PASSION

Copyright © 1989 by
The C.S.S. Publishing Company, Inc.
Lima, Ohio

Library of Congress Cataloging-in-Publication Data

Grimbol, William R., 1950-
    Parents of the passion.

    1. Lent. 2. Worship programs. 3. Monologues.
I. Title.
BV85.G74   1989   264   88-26294
ISBN 1-55673-100-1

9811 / ISBN 1-55673-100-0   PRINTED IN U.S.A.

Table of Contents

Dedication

For Hedy and Lenny, my mother and father,
for teaching me to live my life with
passion and compassion.

Part One

Order of Service: **"Parenting for Honesty"**

Monolog: *"The Mother of Thomas"*

Parenting for Honesty

The Prelude

The Call to Worship

Leader: We come here this [day/night], knowing how often our parenting is built on falsehood.

People: **We are deeply aware that we seldom claim our true feelings . . . our true convictions . . . our true faith.**

Leader: We are aware of how easy it is to conform to the falsehoods of the world.

All: **Free us this [day/night] to celebrate the honest Truth. Amen**

The Opening Hymn "Be Thou my Vision"

The Litany of Confession

Leader: We ask our children to tell us what they feel.

People: **We hide from our children, that which we feel, especially those feelings that make us human.**

Leader: We ask our children to share their questions.

People: **We seldom share our own questions, and often act as if we have all the answers.**

Leader: We ask our children to tell us the Truth.

People: **We often tell them what we think will make them proud, or what they want to hear.**

Leader: We tell our children that faith is important.

People: **We live our daily lives as if faith was the farthest thing from our minds.**

All: **Help us, O God, to be honest with our kids!**

The Assurance of Pardon

The Scripture Lesson 1 John 1:5-10

The Anthem

The Monolog

A Time for Silent Meditation

The Special Creed

> All: We believe in the importance of honesty within our homes, and as the core of all of our family relationships. We choose to celebrate honestly the feelings that make us human. We claim our hurt, our need, our pain, our fear, our wishes and our wants, our dreams and hopes. We know that honesty must first begin by accepting our own fragile human nature. We know that we are created like a piece of crystal, which can shatter at any point. However, if you hold that crystal up to the Light of Christ, it can indeed radiate eternal rainbows.
>
> We believe also in honesty in government, in diplomacy, and within our social institutions. Honesty must be the hallmark of all conduct within the church, for without honesty there can be no community . . . no sense of family . . . no feeling of being the children of God.
>
> We believe in showing honest respect to ourselves, our friends and neighbors, and our God.

The Offering

The Doxology

The Prayer of Dedication

The Lord's Prayer

The Closing Hymn "Lord, Speak to Me, that I May Speak"

The Charge

> Leader: As we leave here this [day/night], let us have a
> renewed dedication to the principles of honesty,
> in order that we might become part of the Light
> and not a part of the Darkness.
>
> All: **We have lived in darkness. We have seen the**
> **Light. Let us choose to follow that Light. Let us**
> **become a part of that Light, the Light which**
> **is the source of all honesty.**

The Benediction

The Postlude

Monolog

The Mother of Thomas

The mother of Thomas is just a trifle eccentric. She is warm, witty, wise. Have fun playing her, and don't be afraid to unleash "the ham" in the characterization.

My kid is the one with the nickname. Sort of a Christ's day version of "Wrong-way Corrigan." Doubting Thomas you call him, which is stupid, and simplistic — and typical, I might add — of the way you folks always have to make the Good News into the Easy News, or the Not-Hard-to-Swallow News, so you brand everything and everyone.

Like Judas. You would think he was the only poor soul in all of history to have betrayed "The One with the Eyes" for a buck. My God, you people do it all the time. Doubting . . . as if he has the corner on the market. Doubting Simon . . . Doubting Andrew . . . Doubting John . . . they *all* doubted, at least until they saw for themselves.

You are all so big on spouting memorized Scripture these days. Gets you off the hook from having to actually *live* it. "They yet believed not." Two of Thomas' comrades saw the Lord while walking in the country. When they had returned from the walk, they told the others *exactly* what they had seen. And what did the others do? They doubted . . . "they yet believed not." Nicknames stink.

Thomas got his doubting from his father. His father was a good man, if you like the rigid, legalistic, inflexible types. And I know that Thoms inherited that factual mind of his from his law-addicted father. I mean really, Abe just would not move without checking the Torah first. It made me so irritable, I just wanted to *spit*. (But he probably would have found a curse for *that* too!)

Being a woman, I never got to know Torah, and for all
the rules and regulations that seem to pour out of it, I'm glad
I missed out on the chance. I really got sick of washing
plates, and I can't *tell* you how many meals were ruined wait-
ing for him to go through that ceremonial washing . . . one
finger at a time. It made me want to serve him pork.
(She looks heavenward) Sorry.

Well, anyway, Thomas certainly got a saturation in the
facts . . . the Law, and I don't think the Resurrection quite
fit into his father's game plan. I think his father would just
have stood there . . . at the Resurrection, that is. I wasn't
there, but everyone talked about it constantly, as much as
the last time the sun went out for a spot . . . all black, and
red rimmed . . . spooky. Thomas' father would have stood
there and just been bored. I can hear Abe now: "Torah never
said this would happen, so it *just did not happen*. It is the
work of the devil." Always fascinated me how many good
people and good things are attributed to the devil.

If I hadn't seen "The Eyes" for myself, well, I would think
that that devil was the only thing that put a bit of passion
and spark, a little drama and flare in this whole Life thing
. . . a little pizzazz.

Thomas, you see, was a trained doubter, for the only
Truth came from Torah, and as you know, "The Eyes" actually turned Torah all inside out . . . sort of a collision of
worlds.

Thomas may not have known immediately that "Eyes"
was in fact the Christ, or the for-real Messiah, but he did
have enough "internal smarts" to know that "Eyes" wasn't
the devil . . . even though he sure spiced up Life a lot too
. . . in fact, some people called "Eyes" the salt of the earth
. . . (smiling) which he was . . . basic, pure — and he gave
Life some taste . . . some meaning . . . some worth.

Salt of the earth. Yep. He even kept us all from rotting
inside.

Now, as for Thomas' faith, his loyalty, well, he got that from me. *(Shrugs and spreads her hands, grinning.)* So modesty is a virtue I missed. He *did* get it from me though. The day he decided to leave and follow "Eyes" . . . had it not been for Abe and the other children, well, I would have been right there with him. I only met Him once . . . Thomas introduced us . . . I had been following them whenever I could, or whenever they didn't stray too far . . . my, they loved to walk *(throw hands in the air)*. I think I was embarrassing to Thomas, but "Eyes" seemed to like me.

I have to admit, "Eyes" wasn't exactly the kind of Messiah I had heard about, but I knew . . . I knew he was the One the first time I waded into those eyes. Eyes reveal the character of a man or woman . . . they reveal the spirit and the soul . . . the fire in the hearth. Jesus' eyes were sometimes wild and smoldering, like the day he got so enraged by the rip-off artists at the Temple. It was wonderful . . . tables flying, doves loose everywhere, shocked men standing with their mouths open wide like the beak of a baby bird at feeding time . . . Or, sometimes his eyes were as sad as a setting sun — peaceful and calm, but knowing somehow that something is over, finished, gone.

Other times his eyes laughed and laughed and laughed. I watched him at a wedding once. The man knew how to have a good time. Too good, Abe thought. And he had eyes that just burst with enthusiasm for all of Life — the love, the family, the friends, the rejoicing — all of it.

Eyes. His eyes told me the Truth. "Eyes." That's one nickname I think I can live with. *(She tilts her head philosophically.)* So, I guess not *every* nickname automatically stinks!

Abe was furious when Thomas left. He chanted and prayed and made enough racket to wake the dead. He made Job sound like the eternal optimist. For three years I had to live with my husband moaning and groaning, wailing and complaining, that his son . . . *his son* . . . was following a false god. I knew the minute I found out that "Eyes" didn't care about plates or washings or not working on the Sabbath — *(wryly)* every woman with children still works on the Sabbath — I knew then that he wasn't a false god. I knew that he would focus in on the things that matter . . . the things which every mother knows really count . . . the mercy, the tenderness, the forgiveness, the hope. It did not surprise me that it was *women* who recognized him first, when he was out of the tomb. Women just know, and I knew he was exactly who he *said* he was.

I heard a story about my son that made me very proud. Jesus wanted to travel to see his good friend Lazarus, now deceased. Some felt he should have gone earlier, before Lazarus died, but the trip to Bethany meant going through Jerusalem. Jerusalem was not exactly the place where "Eyes" was most popular. In fact, the people of Jerusalem had threatened to stone "Eyes" twice before.

I heard that Jesus announced to the twelve that Lazarus was dead and then said to them, "Let us go into Judea again." The person who told me the story, and she is well worth trusting, said that Thomas said, "Let us also go, that we may die with him." I get goosebumps even just saying those words. Thomas, *my* Thomas, knew that the chances were high that a trip through Jerusalem would lead to death for "Eyes" and the whole bloody band of twelve.

My Thomas was a man of courage . . . loyalty . . . compassion . . . conviction, *not just doubt.*

I hate that you just remember his doubt, and not his faith . . . that remarkable faith of his. You know, I believe the reason that "Eyes" never condemned Thomas for his doubts — he never laughed at Thomas, or said, "Thomas, you are being absurd . . . ridiculous" — was that "Eyes" knew that those of us who struggle through the wilderness of our uncertainties usually come out with the stronger and deeper faith.

"Eyes" let Thomas feel his wounds not only because He knew how human it was to doubt, but, I believe, because He knew what an incredibly deep faith Thomas actually had . . . He knew what a mixture of belief and unbelief is every doubt . . . He knew that Thomas would eventually prove his loyalty once again.

Thomas' faith . . . it comes from me. I sowed the seeds. I gave him the ability to "see on the inside" of a man, and in the case of Jesus, what he saw was Life and love itself. Thomas' faith was my creation . . . *(looking heavenward)* sorry . . . I have to say a lot . . . the devil makes me do it . . . *(She laughs and waves as she departs.)*

Part Two

Order of Service: **"Parenting for Hope"**

Monolog: *"The Father of Simon the Zealot"*

Parenting for Hope

The Prelude

The Call to Worship

Leader: We come here this [day/night] wondering how our hope could have evaporated.

People: **We feel foolish clinging to a materialistic — or even a militaristic — hope.**

Leader: It feels hollow to be without hope, and Life loses its point and purpose.

All: **Free us, O Christ, to find our hope in you. Amen**

The Opening Hymn "My Hope is Built on Nothing Less"

The Litany of Confession

Leader: As parents we have too often placed our trust and our hope in worldly wisdom.

People: **Forgive us, O God, for teaching our children to care more for the good life, than for goodness.**

Leader: As parents we have too often guided our children into the ways of the world, the paths of power.

People: **Forgive us, O God, for our lack of faith, a faith that would free us to guide our children to you.**

Leader: As parents we have often taught our children to place their hope in "things," in fame and fortune.

People: **Forgive us, O God, for our failure to build our homes on the foundation of your grace.**

Leader: As parents we have forgotten that real hope comes to those who choose to build the Kingdom.

People: **Forgive us, O God, for choosing instead to build monuments to our own egos.**

All: **Fogive us, O God, for choosing a shallow faith, a faith that yields an empty hope.**

The Assurance of Pardon

The Scripture Lesson Matthew 6:19-34

The Anthem

The Monolog

A Time for Silent Meditation

The Special Creed

> All: We believe that we must teach our children to find hope in You, that they must be filled with a passionate desire to know Your wishes and Your will for their lives.
>
> We believe that we must create within our children a wisdom aware that hope is not the result of fantasy nor idle dreaming, but the product of lives lived with the purpose drawn from your own life.
>
> We believe in a hope that is made possible by choosing You; choosing Your narrow paths; following Your persecuted example; claiming Your crucified Truth.

The Offering

The Doxology

The Prayer of Dedication

The Lord's Prayer

The Closing Hymn "He Leadeth Me, O Blessed Thought"

The Charge

Leader: We must have hope if we are to live fully, and our hope must be fully in you, Lord, if it is to make a genuine difference in all of our tomorrows.

All: **Give us the strength to choose a hope grounded in being Your disciples, for then our hope is certain.**

The Benediction

The Postlude

Monolog

The Father of Simon the Zealot

The father of Simon is sober, objective, despondent, and primarily resigned. There should be a residue of sadness left from every word that this man utters. Simon's father is the living symbol of despair — a good man who has accomplished nothing for the good.

We never really got along all that well.
We hardly ever talked.
We rarely expressed any love for one another . . .
I suppose that is my fault . . . I mean, I never taught him to show affection, and I was the adult, the parent. He was always so intense . . . so argumentative . . . so damn self-righteous. Simon was always involved in some cause, or on some holy crusade.

He alienated most of his family with all his radical and revolutionary ideas. At first I could understand his opposition to Rome. We *all* were, deep down, opposed to Rome. Every Jew quietly despised their rule and their ways. But that was the difference: Simon was never, *ever* quiet. He was a fanatic about his opposition to Rome. He was forever telling you of the history — the history that served as the catalyst for his status — amply earned, I might add — as a Zealot. First, he would always drone on and on about the atrocities of Antiochus Epiphanes, and how Antiochus intended to slaughter a hog on the altar of the holy of holies at the Temple in Jerusalem. He always told the story as if he was the first to have ever heard it, or as if his repugnance was that of the entire Jewish race.

Then, of course, we would hear about the Maccabees, the freedom-fighters, and how Mattathias spoke at the brink of death: "And now, my children, be zealous for the law and give your lives for the covenant of your fathers."

Simon was indeed zealous, and like the other Zealots, his religion was his politics, and vice versa. His religion was a holy war against an oppressive Rome. His religion was that Israel was governed solely by God. He would end this holy harangue with the saga of Masada . . . about the Roman General Titus, and how he was sent to Jerusalem to quell another of the myriad uprisings led by the Zealots . . . about how Titus went on to Masada, and there found in the fortress built by Herod, 1,000 dead Zealots . . . to a man they had taken their own lives rather than be captured by the hated Romans.

Simon would say this last part with an intense earnestness and sincerity. There was no question that he found the whole Zealot movement and cause to be a godly one, for he always spoke as if he had God right there at his side. One could never doubt that Simon believed.

As you probably have guessed by now, I was too mild . . . too middle-of-the-road for my son. He never so much as called me a collaborator with Rome, but he *did* often tell me of the Sicarii, and how these hard-core Zealots assassinated any Jew thought to be someone who compromised with the Roman authorities, or who entered into any treaty or agreement with them. I would ask him if he was warning me, but he always said he wasn't, and just wanted to keep me informed. I was informed. We were *all* informed. In fact, every Jew alive was suspicious of every other Jew. We never knew when one of us would be thought to be a conspirator with Rome, or when we would be branded as a traitor to our race . . .our people . . . our faith.

I guess I was a moderate. At least, I was in Simon's eyes. I never took a clear-cut stand, or voiced any strong objection in public, or attacked Roman rule in any substantive or significant way.

I agreed with much of what he said, but I chose a different path. I chose a path that I could live with . . . that my family could live with . . . that would allow me to continue to live and work in my home town.

Simon was free. He had no obligations or responsibilities to anyone, except himself. He could do and say whatever he pleased, and the only one to suffer was Simon. He wasn't a husband. He wasn't a father. He didn't really care what his own parents thought of what he did.

He was free to be a fanatic.

I could not travel such a reckless road as he did. I just had too much to lose and too many people counting on me . . . counting on me to survive.

It really came as no shock then, when he took up with that Jesus character. I mean, talk about a fanatic . . .a zealot . . . a revolutionary . . . a radical! *Well,* he was the personification of all of that. The only thing that even sent a ripple of a surprise through me, was that Simon could have a Roman tax collector as one of his close colleagues. Imagine *that!* Here was my son, Mr. Anti-Rome, and here he offers allegiance to someone who could so flagrantly violate the very same Law to which the Zealots were supposedly so violently committed. I say I was only mildly surprised, because I had learned long ago, that fanatics are like the spring winds which blow crisp and cold, and then blow soft and balmy.

Simon always had an explanation, and for this too he had a well-thought-out defense plan. We encountered each other one day in the hills, on one of the few occasions I ever saw him alone. On that occasion he said that he now knew that the Law and his anti-Roman zeal had been consumed in a wider, nobler, more mature vision. He loved using the word "mature" on me. He claimed it was a vision of a Kingdom, the Messianic Kingdom, and that this Jesus was indeed the man of whom John the Baptizer preached. I told him that I found it hard to comprehend how the Messiah who was the "author" of the Law, would somehow now decide to defy it, or that it was now suddenly okay to be a cohort with a Roman collaborator.

Simon, as was always the case when he did not know, simply said I could never understand. He was right on that one.

I never saw him again. At the end of that conversation, we just stood staring at each other coldly, and a black chasm existed between us, a chasm we would never cross. We never said good-bye. We just walked away from each other. He went back to Him. I went back to my family and my work. Ironic, but the winds that day blew hot and cold, all in a whirl. I felt so hollow inside, I could have . . .

I am weary of it all.

I am bored to tears with my son's enflamed scruples.

I am sick to death of prophets who come and declare that the Kingdom is at hand . . . that peace will reign . . . that the first shall be last . . . that the poor will flourish . . . that the sick will be well . . . that the Truth will win.

They come and they go.

The poor are still poor.

War, more than righteousness and justice, flows like the rivers . . . rivers of blood and hate and tears.

A miracle or two, maybe, but most of the sick still die.

The last are still last.

The first are still first.

The idealism of Simon makes me want to wretch.

The Truth has never won, and it never will. I don't believe the world was made to handle the Truth, or to have the Truth growing up in the midst of this stale and stinking earth.

All of the Zealots . . . all of the disciples . . . all of that faith, and everything is still the silly same.

What a fitting tribute is the cross. The place where hope died. The place where Truth gets nailed up again in anguish.

The saddest part is that now they run around like lunatics, claiming that He is still alive. If He is, so what? Nothing ever changes, really. Even if we were fools enough to even believe He was still around, well, what would it change? What difference would it make?

I am weary of it all. I do my job. I am a good husband. I am a good — except for Simon — father. I have a good reputation. I believe in the Law . . . God . . . my people. Most would say that I am a very good man.

Still, I missed receiving the one thing I wanted most . . . to have Simon say, just once, that he respected me. Why should Simon's respect mean so much? Why, crazy as it may seem, because of all the people I have ever met, I respected Simon the most. Across the chasm burned an admiration that could scorch a star. I wish I could have told him. I was just too tired to even try . . . too sick of defending myself . . . too sick of his arrogance.

He tells me that Jesus is a forgiving Lord. I hope his Lord will forgive him his pompous faith, and his lack of honor for his father. I hope he can forgive me for playing it safe. I just have so many obligations and duties, so many people counting on me, my reputation . . .

I am just so weary of it all.

Part Three

Order of Service: **"Parenting for Courage"**

Monolog: *"The Mother of Nathanael"*

Parenting for Courage

The Prelude

The Call to Worship

> Leader: We gather here this [day/night], as a people in need of firming up our faith . . .
> **People: And firming up our families.**
> Leader: As we worship together, enable us to be seized by Your Spirit . . .
> **All: A spirit that is full to overflowing with Your calling. Amen**

The Opening Hymn "God of Grace and God of Glory"

The Litany of Confession

> Leader: As parents we have often encouraged conformity . . .
> **People: Rather than discipleship.**
> Leader: As parents we have often encouraged following rules . . .
> **People: Even when those rules kept us from following Christ.**
> Leader: Forgive us, O Christ, for being obedient to the whims of the culture . . .
> **People: Rather than being a slave to the vision of Christ, a vision of the Kingdom of God.**
> Leader: Forgive us, O God, for our passion for safety, and our deep desire to always fit in.
> **People: Forgive us for raising our children to be "winners," even when the price of victory is their soul.**
> **All: Grant us the courage to be the disciples You created us to be. Amen**

The Assurance of Pardon

The Scripture Lesson Romans 12:1, 2, 9-21

The Anthem

The Monolog

A Time for Silent Meditation

The Special Creed

> All: We believe in the courage to be true to our God-created selves. We believe in the courage to serve . . . to suffer . . . to sacrifice. We believe in the courage to follow the Christ, and the wisdom of choosing the road less traveled.
>
> We believe in the courage to preach good news to the poor, and to know that this requires of us the active support and pursuit of justice in our world. We believe in justice as the guiding political and economic principle of God's world.
>
> We believe in the courage to make peace . . . with our selves . . . our neighbors . . . our enemies . . . our God. We see Jesus Christ as the igniter of all true courage, and the spark of all genuine bravery.

The Offering

The Doxology

The Prayer of Dedication

The Lord's Prayer

The Closing Hymn "Stand Up, Stand Up for Jesus"

The Charge

> Leader: Let us go from this place with courage, the courage to pick up our crosses . . .
>
> **All:** **And follow him who is our Lord and our Savior. Let us be about building the Kingdom.**

The Benediction

The Postlude

Monolog

The Mother of Nathanael

Nathanael's mother has an enormous heart. She reflects a spirit of great honesty and emotional integrity. She is a woman in grief — raw absorbing and thoroughly penetrating grief. She is a woman surrounded by people, especially family and friends, but who is still very much alone. In many ways, she is like every mother everywhere.

I walk about his room at night. I listen for his voice everywhere. Often I think I have seen him at the market, or that I have caught a glimpse of him walking down a street. At times, at late night, I come into his room, and I sit on his bed . . . and I listen to the moaning of the stars, or to the gentle caress of the rain on the roof, or to the wild wailing wind.

I sit and listen, and I think, and I think . . . and I pray. I pray with hope . . . and with hopelessness. I think of the times I tucked him into his bed, or sat by him for hours when he was sick. I think of the laughter that came from his belly when he would run and play with the other children.

I think of the tears that fell from his sad sad face the day my father died. They were very much alike, those two — kind . . . gentle . . . compassionate . . . just — in fact, Nathanael's grandfather always said that if Israel were still governed by Judges, Nathanael would have surpassed Samuel in greatness. Those two . . . they walked and talked . . .they fished . . . they argued until they both were as red as a Roman cape.

I think of the way he talked to me, the way he listened. His own father never listened, never seemed to care. But Nathanael would sit with me for hours, and listen. I would talk . . . he would listen. It's funny, but I hardly recall what

I talked about. Everything I guess, or maybe nothing. But
. . . but . . . it just felt so good to talk, and to be *heard*.
Whenever I had finished rambling on about his brothers and
sisters, or the synagogue, or the Romans, or Moses, or what
I was making for dinner, or my plans for his brilliant future
. . . well, he would always stand up and touch my cheek,
and then he would laugh a kind little laugh, a laugh with
no malice . . . and he would always say, "Mama, you are
precious. God takes such pride in you." Imagine that! From
a *son* no less. Such pride in me. It made me feel like bursting with tears and smiles and laughter, and God knows what
else.

That gentle laugh . . . a face so sweet . . . a touch so
tender . . . I know. I can imagine you are thinking I'm just
another sentimental old lady, just another proud Jewish
mother, an adoring Mama. No, I have seven other children,
and I have been around so many more, I cannot count them
all.

But Nathanael was different . . . so different. He was just
so . . . Sentimentalism would cheapen this, so please don't
just call me sentimental. I mean, "sentimental" is our human brand for everything that makes us cry, everything that
makes us feel deep hurt. He was just so fine . . . so excellent
. . . so . . . I miss him so . . . I just ache so much inside.

I try to keep from drifting off . . . it is like my whole soul
just sails out the window, off to the hills to find him, and
have a conversation with him. Some days I am just so bit-
ter that my blood feels as cold as water from the deepest
well, and I want to scream and throw things. And at times
I do. My husband tells me I'm silly. He tells me to accept
that he is gone, to get over it, to accept the fact that
Nathanael has disowned us, and that he will never ever be
welcome in this home again.

I can't! I can't let go. I can't say goodbye. He is still alive.
He is still out there, and someone is still receiving that gentle touch, and that little laugh. He is out there listening.

If he came back, I would run to meet him. I would squeeze him with all of my might. He didn't disown me . . . I am precious . . . God takes pride in me . . . he calls me Mama . . . he would never disown me. I know he says we are no longer his parents, but it is this Jesus who has him so confused, who has gotten him so totally mixed up. I am precious . . . Mama . . . God's pride . . . he would never disown me.

I hate . . . I despise this man Jesus. I loathe all of his rubbish about love. What does *he* know about "love"? What does he know about the love of a parent? He takes our children away from us. He leads them out into the world preaching some nonsense about how the first will be last, about releasing captives, about the Kingdom coming now.

Good boys, like my Nathanael, are taken in by this holy song and dance, this miracle message. Miracle? Why, it has been heard from every prophet from the beginning of time.

Jesus talks love. He *preaches* love, but he sows hate and discord. He breaks up whole families, and he leaves us — he leaves *me* — with an empty room, an empty bed.

Nobody to listen to me . . . no touch . . . no laugh . . . no feeling precious. I despise the ground that he walks on.

How could a Messiah bring so much pain, so much agony? How could a Messiah bring such upset to our family, the family which is the foundation of faith, and of Life itself? How could a Messiah take away my Nathanael, and have him showing more love to lepers and prostitutes and beggars . . . more love . . . more love than he shows to me . . . his mother, the same mother Torah teaches to honor and obey? Honor? Obey? Jesus wants all of that for himself!

Jesus, if you can hear me . . . let me go . . . let my Nathanael go. You know where you are headed. You know exactly what you are doing . . . riding into town on the back of an ass . . . proclaiming to be the Messiah in the midst of the holy days . . . the sacred "season" of our faith. You are taking these young men on a long cruel trail, a trail to nowhere. A trail to a cross . . . I am certain. Haven't you caused us all enough grief already? Haven't you inflicted enough pain on all twelve families? Twelve? Yes, all twelve must feel as I do, that you needed comfort and support for your crazy cause, that you did not have the courage to do it alone, and so you recruited our sons with your charisma . . . and your seductive massage of saving the world . . . building the kingdom.

What? What will you build from a cross? What kind of Messiah would be crucified? You are a charlatan, Jesus . . . a fake. Let my Nathanael go.

I have heard that you said of my son, "Behold an Israelite indeed, in whom is no guile." True Jesus, but what about you? What about the cunning . . . the deceit . . . the fraud of who *you* are? Miracles . . . healings . . . prophesies of a new Kingdom . . . a new way of life for all . . . forgiveness for all . . . I have heard your message . . . I have heard it a million times in my lifetime, my one single solitary lifetime.

Jesus, you will be nailed up, and you will leave those young men in total despair . . . wondering where the Kingdom has gone . . . wondering why the poor are still so poor, and why the blind still cannot see, or the lame walk, or why we will continue to fight war after crazy war. You are headed for destruction, and you know it, and yet, you will not tell the Truth to these young men.

Guile. Guile? You are correct, my Nathanael does not have any. But you, Jesus, you have enough for all twelve. Won't you please let them all go now, before you upset any more people? Before they stone you, or crucify you? Or . . . or . . . (screaming) Jesus, if they should kill my son for the likes of you . . . if they should kill my Nathanael, I will pray that you rot in the pits of hell . . . I will pray without ceasing, and I will be heard!

(She speaks more calmly.) Stop . . . in the name of God . . . stop. It is so futile, so worthless. Nothing will change, you will see. Please, let him go . . . please . . . please . . .

Part Four

Order of Service: **"Parenting for Love"**

Monolog: *"The Father of Peter"*

Parenting for Love

The Prelude

The Call to Worship

Leader: We come here this [day/night], fully aware of how often we have failed to make loving our top priority, our most important work.

People: **Fill this time of worship, O God, with a deep sense of the love we feel for one another, as friends, and as the family of faith.**

Leader: Remind us all that loving is the call of Christ, and that loving forms the core of discipleship. Free us to follow him who is the Author of Love.

All: **Bond us together this day in the spirit of love. Amen**

The Opening Hymn "Love Divine, All Loves Excelling"

The Litany of Confession

Leader: Too often we forget to teach the art of loving.

People: **We are consumed in teaching our children how to make a living, how to "make it big."**

Leader: Too often we fail to work at loving in our own homes.

People: **We allow our homes to become hotels where strangers pass in the halls.**

Leader: Too often we neglect our own friendships.

People: **We think we can be self-sufficient, or that deep friendship just takes too much effort.**

Leader: Too often we do no more than talk about loving.

People: **We need to show our love through our listening, our compassion, our forgiveness.**

All: **In a world that seems only to celebrate romance, let us be a people dedicated to the real work of love. Amen**

The Assurance of Pardon

The Scripture Lesson 1 Corinthians 13

The Anthem

The Monolog

A Time for Silent Meditation

The Special Creed

All: We believe that to love is our greatest calling in life, as well as our most significant responsibility. We understand loving to be the most difficult and most rewarding work of life.

We believe that all true loving is grounded in the love of Jesus Christ, and that when we see another human being through his eyes, love will fairly flow from us.

We believe that true loving includes conflict and pain, honesty and hurt, as well as happiness and genuine joy. We do not believe in a love that is without forgiveness, for every loving relationship requires many fresh starts.

We believe that the church should be about the business of teaching us how to love. It is the church that must inspire us to bind the broken-hearted, and to reach out to the outcast, to become the Good Samaritan.

The Offering

The Doxology

The Prayer of Dedication

The Lord's Prayer

The Closing Hymn "O Love That Will Not Let me Go"

The Charge

> Leader: There is no living without loving, and there is no
> life without those who passionately love to live and
> live to love.
>
> **All:** **We are those people. We are those who em-**
> **brace life with the spirit of grace, the uncon-**
> **ditional love of God.**

The Benediction

The Postlude

Monolog

The Father of Peter

The father of Peter is a man's man, but as is often the case with "John Wayne" types, a teddy bear lurks within. He tries hard to be angry, but beneath his feigned rage is a simple and overwhelming sadness and sorrow.

Peter was indeed everything I could have ever hoped for in a son. He was the best. He was dedicated. He was hard working. Why, he could work from dawn to sunset without ever uttering a complaint. Stong? The boy was as strong as an ox. Other fathers would tease their sons about how they compared to my Peter.

He had muscles like small mountains, and he was agile and quick . . . he could maneuver those nets in and out of the water with such grace . . . it was a joy to behold. Believe it or not, other fishermen would come sometimes just to watch . . . to watch him . . . to see how it could be done.

He was our pride and joy all right. Showed us honor and respect at all times. He even cared for his grandmother daily . . . doing chores for her . . . making up for all the little things left undone since my father died. He lived the Law. Prayed. Worshiped. Rested on Sabbath . . . proper diet . . .he understood that the rituals and rules of our faith kept us close to God, in communion with God. He never questioned their wisdom or validity.

Does this sound like bragging? Does it? Well, I suppose it should. I had a lot to brag about. The kid was . . . was, well, a dream come true for any father. He had everything. He had friends by the horde. He was always the life of the party . . . always telling the joke or making the funny face

. . . people loved it. He was also the advisor, my goodness, for the whole town it seemed . . . they all sought out Peter. It was strange the way they would come . . . women with children . . . men twice his age . . . asking about everything from the purpose of Life to how to settle some silly family squabble. It was almost as if Peter was a Samuel or a Gideon. I mean, if our land were still governed by Judges, well, you can bet your life that Peter would have been a Judge known absolutely everywhere.

He just had that magic . . . that charisma . . . (laughing lightly) and his looks didn't hurt him any either. He was handsome. Awkward for another man to say such things, but Peter was a very handsome young man.

I have lost him . . . my Peter . . . lost him. We have not spoken a word in two and one half years . . . almost a thousand days. A thousand days! I have no idea what happened. I will never understand. I will not accept

(His anger is rising) I will not forgive him for . . . for the pain and the humiliation he has caused me, for the pain and hurt and worry which has infested his mother's soul . . . her face has never been the same since the day he left. She never smiles. She never scurries about the house . . . preparing meals . . . readying for the Sabbath . . . straightening or cleaning . . . or visiting with the other women of the village. She is a shell now . . . hollow . . . and my marriage is the same. We have no marriage. When I touch her . . . my own wife . . . she recoils like I am a deadly serpent, as if it is somehow my fault.

He has killed us both.

I cannot forgive.

It makes no sense even to his friends, and I have talked with every close friend he has ever had . . . to try to find some clue . . . to try to make something within this fog come into focus. Everyone is baffled. Some say he is possessed. Some say that he just got caught up in the tide of this man Jesus' power. Well, I for one just cannot believe that.

Peter is not a *follower* — he is a *leader*. People *came* to him. I cannot accept the notion that my powerful Peter got swept up by just another wayward prophet! I cannot accept it!

His friends say that he talks incessantly about some new Kingdom . . . about how there will finally be peace, and that all wars will cease . . . all people will be fed . . . the lepers will be accepted . . . cleansed . . . the prostitutes and robbers will be changed and forgiven . . . greed will disappear . . . lust will vanish . . . adultery . . . gone . . . all sin gone . . . (He breaks into loud cackling laughter.) My God, how could my Peter fall prey to such garbage . . . to such idealistic rubbish? How could my Peter ever swallow such an idiotic notion that this Kingdom could exist without a Messiah?

That is the other mystery . . . the other puzzle part. His friends say Peter clearly believes this Jesus *is* the Messiah. The Messiah? Peter . . . how can you believe that a man just like all of us . . . a man with no distinction . . . a man who will die as surely as I will . . . how can you believe him to be the Messiah?

Peter, do you actually *see* this Kingdom? Where is it? Where? Do you *see* it in the streets filled with beggars, or on the battlefields that are still everywhere? Where *is* this Kingdom? A healing . . . a miracle you say . . . a powerful parable . . . and that is enough for you? That gives you enough to proclaim the Kingdom . . . the Messiah?

Your mother once told me that when she used to go to tuck you in bed, to give you a kiss good night, you would want her to find you a wishing star. Every night, even on the cloudy ones, she would point out the window in your room to some star, pretend or real, and she would say to you, "Peter, there is your star, now make a wish, and then go to sleep." She told me, Peter, that you always wished for everyone to be happy . . . to have enough food and clothes . . . and to have good parents like you had. Peter . . . your mother and I always thought it odd for a young boy to make such wishes. Is that it, Peter? Are you still wishing on a star?

Your mother says that you also told her that there must be more to life than just fishing. You never once spoke these words to me. I suppose you knew that I would reject them, or that the thought of there being something more than fishing, well, that this might hurt me. But you told your mother that some day you were going to figure out everything in the world.

You were six, Peter.

Six years old . . . and you wanted happy people, and answers. Only six.

Peter . . . I hope you have found your star, but I am afraid, Peter, that the sky is very cloudy tonight, and the star, Peter, the star is just pretend. Come home, son.

Peter, I have been told that he has told you that you will be the rock upon which he will build his church. The rock. You *are* a rock, Peter . . . you are strong inside and out . . . you are a leader . . . a born leader . . . you deserve that role, that responsibility, for you will be the foundation of *any* church that Jesus is able to create on this earth. I hope he knows that he has, in you, the very best, Peter. I hope he knows that he has the very best. I miss you, son . . . I really miss you. One thousand days. One thousand . . .

Peter . . . I wonder if you have finally found that star, but Peter, do you know . . . do you have any idea how hard it will be to follow that star? To remain true to your wish? Do you know how frightening a cross can be? Do you know the dangers of this Kingdom which you preach? Do you know the price you might have to pay? Do you know what might become of Jesus?

Peter, are you *really* ready to swear total devotion? It will be so hard . . . so brutal . . . you will need all of your strength, Peter . . . all of it. You are only human, Peter . . . only one man . . . only one. A rock, yes. But the road will be so tough . . . so tough. I wish you well, Peter . . . I wish you well.

Part Five

Order of Service: **"Parenting for Faith"**

Monolog: *"The Mother of Judas"*

Parenting for Faith

The Prelude

The Call to Worship

Leader: We come here this [day/night] with a fragile faith.
People: **Create in us, O God, a faith of strength and stamina.**
Leader: Our faith needs the embrace of your grace.
All: **Squeeze out of us, O Christ, all doubt, and let us celebrate together a full, firm faith. Amen.**

The Opening Hymn "My Faith Looks Up to Thee"

The Litany of Confession

Leader: We neglect our faith by failing to serve others.
People: **Free us to become living sacrifices in Your name.**
Leader: We abuse our faith by failing to be disciplined — in our prayer life and in our worshiping.
People: **Enable us, O Christ, to make time with you a top priority of each and every day.**
Leader: We use our faith as a wall of answers, keeping ourselves from learning and maturing.
People: **Keep our faith active and alive, filled with questions and the search for truth.**
Leader: We allow our faith to corrode whenever we become consumed in consuming.
People: **Allow our faith to be the treasure it was always intended to be, and the key to our heart.**
All: **Create in us a faith that is devoted to You, and You alone. Amen**

The Assurance of Pardon

The Scripture Lesson   Hebrews 11:1-6, 32-40; 12:1, 2

The Anthem

The Monolog

The Time for Silent Meditation

The Special Creed

All: We affirm a faith that is free . . . free to question and to doubt . . . free to serve and to sacrifice . . . free to follow.

We affirm a faith that is unafraid . . . of questions and questioning . . . of challenges and changes . . . of building a Kingdom of justice, equality and peace.

We affirm a faith that is loyal . . . obedient to Your will and wish for our lives . . . enslaved by Your Spirit . . . aware that You are our very best friend.

We affirm a faith that is transforming . . . always new . . . always forgiving . . . always becoming . . . always freeing us to face the day with a new perspective and a positive purpose.

We affirm a faith that is a celebration . . . of the Truth . . . of dedication and devotion . . . of the joy of discipleship . . . of the hope of the Kingdom to come.

The Offering

The Doxology

The Prayer of Dedication

The Lord's Prayer

The Closing Hymn "What a Friend We Have in Jesus"

The Charge

> Leader: When our faith is full, our hearts and minds open to the Truth, we will seize each day as a magnificent gift.
>
> All: **We leave here this day, ready to cherish this moment as a miracle, ready to feel all the mystery and magic that saturates each new dawn.**

The Benediction

The Postlude

Monolog

The Mother of Judas

This is a counter-culture character, a true bleeding heart liberal, for Judas' mother believed her God calls everyone to let their hearts bleed on behalf of the oppressed. She is a woman possessed of great warmth, wit, and wisdom, and she is eminently likeable. She is intelligent, and intellectually sharp. She is a strong, competent, and yet motherly advocate for true legacy of her son.

Our home was always filled with the misfits and the castoffs. I don't know why that was. I just never questioned having my door open. I guess that was just my faith. My table was always open. We shared everything that we ate, everything that we owned. At times during Passover, there would be people sleeping from one end of the house to the other . . . wall to wall . . . bodies everywhere. I think Judas always thought his family was like the weather, always changing . . . different numbers . . . different complexions and colors . . . all ages . . . and I mean to tell you — all types.

I make no bones about it, I've hid a robber or two . . . or three . . . so, who is counting . . . from the authorities. Authorities . . . I've always hated authorities. Even as a little girl, the thought of them made me want to kick them in the shins. Anyone telling me what to do . . . except mother and father (and even *them* sometimes) . . . I just didn't go for that stuff.

Judas always laughed when I would talk to the authorities at the door, with a thief hidden in the loft, or under blankets or wherever . . . "No sir, I've not seen a soul all day . . . no I've not heard anything. I've been praying most of the day, sir, coming closer to God. What did he look like?

No, never saw anyone look like that. But then, as I said, I've been spending my time here in quiet, humble meditation. Yes sir, I'll report to you immediately if I see him. I'm a good citizen. Will do. Will do. Right away. You bet." (She roars with laughter as she slams an imaginary door shut.) Judas would laugh his head off after they had left, and then he would applaud.

As for the robber or the thief or the whatever, well, I would tell him simply that God had obviously forgiven his sinful behind, and that the next time he would not be so lucky to have a good neighbor to keep him out of prison — or off a cross, for that matter. I'd always feed them before they left, and say a prayer . . . a long, guilt-laden one. Judas liked the adventure of all this, all of the excitement and drama . . . he loved the rebelliousness of it all.

Well, he sure did have a rebel for a mother. I guess I was never the type that did what the good people were supposed to do . . . which was nothing worth anything anyway. Good people never seemed real good to me. Good people lead boring, predictable lives. "Good folks," at least the religious elite around here, are so smug and arrogant that they have no time to care about anyone or anything. You would think they had never heard God's call to feed the poor, or give shelter, or protect the widow. They live for themselves . . . always have, always will. "Good" folks . . . no goodness whatsoever. I'm not saying I'm good, but I do know that God wants charity to all, and charity means justice, and justice means equality, and equality was my home . . . one big happy family. What a collection we were . . . a real bouquet of weeds and thorns, with a flower or two thrown in for a splash of color.

Judas' father never complained. He'd shake his head sometimes, but he agreed with me. Or, if he didn't agree, he at least loved me enough to let me be. He always said that Judas was just like me. And he was: same heart, same needs; he loved people, all kinds, just like me; and he hated — despised — injustice. And what a *temper!* That boy would explode whenever he saw an injustice of any kind. He sure got into some bad fights defending his convictions. I remember one time he befriended a Samaritan. He lost every other friend he had. So he told his "friends" they were worthless to him . . . worthless if they could not accept this Samaritan boy. That Samaritan child, Josiah, was his very best friend even until the day he died. He was close to the other disciples, but these two were like brothers . . . *brothers.* I guess maybe only Jesus meant as much to Judas.

I was never shocked by his decision to follow Jesus. Jesus just took our home on the road. I liked Jesus. He was smart . . . sensitive . . . had a wonderful way with children . . . and he made sense. I don't know if he was the Messiah. I really don't care much. I mean, the Messiah . . . the Kingdom . . . that's just stuff for the good folks to talk about . . . argue about . . . feel self-righteous about.

All I know is, that I know Truth when I *see* it, and I know Truth when I *hear* it. But most of all, I know Truth when I *feel* it — *inside.* Jesus and Judas brought a lot of Truth to this world. Messiah? Who really cares? People got fed . . . people got healed . . . that's what matters. People with a little food and a little hope in their bellies, now *that* I can believe in. Yes, indeed.

I wasn't shocked by Judas' betrayal either. I know my Judas, and when he saw Jesus wasting . . . wasting that precious ointment, letting that woman waste that costly nard . . . well, I know my Judas. He would have been enraged. He would have felt betrayed by Jesus . . . I mean, Jesus was repudiating everything he had ever said, and everything Judas had ever learned at home. I never wasted a thing. I never allowed luxury in our home. I never ever indulged myself, or my family. Judas was the same.

This wasted ointment? Pure indulgence! I'm sure Judas was convinced his friend was now just another prophetic charlatan, and that he had been duped . . . fooled. And *that* would make Judas explode. No, I understand the betrayal. Judas gave up on Jesus, just as Jesus had obviously given up on the poor. At least, that's the way I see it.

I wasn't shocked by the suicide either. I know Judas never believed that the cross was really just around the corner. Judas just never believed that justice would be met by pure, raw injustice . . . hate. Judas had no idea that his friend Jesus would be so victimized . . . so mocked . . . so made the joke of all Jews.

Judas never really caught on to the irony of that ointment, and how it was supposed to prepare his body for death. I'm sure Judas thought he would just expose Jesus for being a charlatan, a phoney prophet . . . but I'm sure he never ever believed that he would kill the Truth . . . *kill* it!

Suicide . . . my Judas could not tolerate his mistake. He had betrayed his friend. He had betrayed the truth. He had failed to realize that Jesus really *did* know his days were numbered. Judas thought their mission would go on and on and on . . . he thought Jesus was just selling out . . . being indulgent. He wanted to make him hurt, to expose Jesus' failure. He never thought the cross . . . he never thought Jesus would die. I know he never thought that. Otherwise, his suicide would make zero sense. He must have loved that man. He *must* have loved him.

My home is still open . . . there's still people everywhere . . . travelers . . . a thief or beggar or prostitite in hiding. And Judas is still there. I can feel his smile in the room. I can hear his laughter. I can sense his presence. He was a good boy . . . and a good man . . . and I'm still proud of him.

Part Six

Order of Service: **"Parenting for Trust"**

Monolog: *"The Father of James the Less"*

Parenting for Trust

The Prelude

The Call to Worship

Leader: We gather this [day/night] knowing that we still want total control of our lives.

People: **The thought of trusting you, O Christ, still strikes us awkward and strange.**

Leader: We need to gain a deeper trust in You, a willingness to turn our lives over to Your care.

All: **Free us, O Christ, to trust in your will. Amen**

The Opening Hymn "I Need Thee Every Hour"

The Litany of Confession

Leader: We constantly seek to be in charge.

People: **Even when we know our lives are out of control.**

Leader: We despise the thought of surrendering.

People: **So we foolishly pretend to be self-sufficient.**

Leader: We do not really know how to let go, and let God.

People: **We still think God helps only those who help themselves.**

Leader: We still do not believe that You can remove our flaws, and failures.

People: **We do not believe that You can transform us.**

All: **Teach us, O Christ, the wisdom of waving the white flag, the genius of trusting solely in you. Amen**

The Assurance of Pardon

The Scripture Lesson John 15:1-17

The Anthem

The Monolog

A Time for Silent Meditation

The Special Creed

All: We believe in maintaining a close and personal relationship to Jesus Christ. We believe that by staying in close communion with "the true vine," we enable ourselves to become people capable of producing good and beautiful lives.

We believe that as we gain a deeper trust in Christ, as our Lord and our Savior, we will find ourselves growing in our trust of self . . . others . . . our world . . . life itself. As we deepen our bond and commitment to Christ, we know that we will experience a profound inner peace, and a powerful spiritual calling.

We understand surrender not to be a sign of weakness, but a testimony to wisdom, the wisdom to know that God and God alone can provide us with the truth and the direction we so desperately seek.

The Offering

The Doxology

The Prayer of Dedication

The Lord's Prayer

The Closing Hymn   "O God, Our Help in Ages Past"

The Charge

> Leader: We are indeed capable of bearing abundant
> fruit, if we simply choose to remain tied to the
> vine.
>
> **All:**   **We trust in our Lord, the True Vine, and
> we find satisfaction and hope in being his
> chosen branches.**

The Benediction

The Postlude

Monolog

The Father of James the Less

*James' father is an intense, serious, reserved man, and a deeply
devoted father. One gains the impression that he is difficult for his
son to reach, somehow emotionally detached, and yet a man whose
love for James is genuine and full. One should also easily recognize
that James came by his awkward shyness honestly, even if his father
has it well covered by his competent and controlled image. Beneath
this cool, calm, collected exterior beats a passionate heart, one filled
with caring and concern for his son.*

My son James never quite fit in. He . . . well . . . he sort
of always fell through the cracks. He's not ugly, but I wouldn't
call him handsome. No, I must admit, he isn't really
handsome.

He isn't stupid, but he isn't really all that smart either.
When the other young boys would talk of hunting or fight-
ing or racing one another, James would just go quiet, painfully quiet.

With girls James was just so shy — painfully shy. Painful
. . . that's how it feels to watch your son be left alone so
often, be so isolated, be so unsure of himself . . . so unhappy.
It hurt me deeply to watch him try so hard to fit in, to make
friends, to be accepted.

At times my heart just ached to watch him watch the
other young men his age laugh and carry on, talking of par-
ties and beautiful women, boasting of strength and their mili-
tary prowess, or how the future was to be filled with their
fame and fortune. James would just sit and stare at them,
silent, so obviously filled with that strange mix of loathing
and envy. Always alone. Always watching and listening. Always staring. Always telling me he wouldn't want to be like
them anyway. Shallow, braggers, he called them. It made

me just want to cry sometimes. You just want your children to be happy, to be accepted, to be liked.

I remember one day when he was about ten or eleven, some of the kids had cornered him in an alleyway and were making him dance. I'm sure they threatened to pulverize the poor kid. He was so scrawny, so shy. And so he danced. He danced for those idiots, and I saw it all as I returned from the market. I yelled at that quartet of mockers to get away from James, but James' eyes told me he wished he could have just finished the dance. Then they would have left him alone — at least for a day or two. He gave them plenty to laugh about. His humiliation was unbearable to watch. My hurt was unbearable to feel. If I could have, I would have killed all four of them, my anger was so intense, my hurt so bloated. A father just dies inside if his son is humiliated like that. You just die . . . you just die. I'll never forget his face that day, and his eyes, those silent sad eyes of his. I will never forget it . . . never . . . never. His eyes were . . . it was awful.

From the day he met Jesus there was a remarkable change in him. It was almost a complete transformation. James suddenly came alive. He had heard this man speak several times before he ever became one of his band, and he would always sound so excited to tell his mother and me about what Jesus had said. I'm not saying I agree with everything this Jesus says, or even does, but there is no denying he was good for James — real good.

I must admit to some envy of Jesus, I mean, I only wish James could love *me* the way he so obviously does Jesus. I've watched them talk for hours, argue for hours, and then hug. And you can see it in James' eyes: Jesus is his friend . . . *his* best friend . . . honestly, his *first* friend. Sometimes I wish I could be that close to him. But I can't. And now he's off and on his own, as it should be, I know.

Still, I wish I could know him as well as I know Jesus must . . . just one hug . . . we've never hugged . . . I've never told the kid how much I love him.

I've heard plenty of others condemn Jesus. I must admit, I don't know if he really is the Messiah or not, but to tell the truth, I don't care. I really don't. He has been good for James — in fact, the whole group has been good for him. He looks happy . . . full of Life . . . full of purpose. My goodness, when we *do* see the kid we can't shut him up! He is just *filled* with stories and tales of their work and their journeys.

I don't know about the miracle stuff. But James is absolutely convinced. Anyway, what harm are they doing? They help so many people . . . they feed folks . . . they offer love to those whom everyone else finds unlovable . . . they offer hope . . . they are gentle . . . kind . . . caring . . . compassionate young men, every one of them.

I just don't see the big controversy, the big conflict. Crucify Him? I mean, how *ridiculous,* For *what?* For being too good? For caring too much? Even if he *isn't* the Messiah, He sure is a breath of fresh air. I just fail to see what harm they are causing. Anyway, I have zero complaints. For James, He had done wonders. I'm sure they won't crucify Him. It will pass over, But what a ridiculous reaction to someone so innocent, so basically good.

It really feels terrific to see my son so happy, satisfied, content. He is finally accepted. He finally has friends. It feels so good to see him so confident. I never thought I would say this about James, but he really is an incredible human being. He really *is*.

He is so just in all his dealings, so fair, and I've been unbelievably impressed by his courage. He speaks his convictions regardless what others think. He stands up for the outcasts . . . the lepers . . . the prostitutes . . . the beggars.

And he just seems to have endless energy. I cannot believe how hard they all work . . . constantly . . . day after day after day. And they live on nothing, just the barest essentials.

I've gone from being a father who genuinely pitied his poor son, to being a father who genuinely admires him. "Admire." I never ever believed I would come to admire James. But I do. With my whole heart. I do.

Like I said, I don't know about that miracle and Messiah stuff. But I do know this: Jesus has been a miracle for James, a Messiah to his Life. Before Jesus, James was just dead — just a lonely, lost, bored young man. To see him now . . . well it's just unbelievable. He's so full of Life . . . so genuine . . . so good . . . he is a genuinely good man. What father could ask for more? What God could ask for more? I'll bet those four boys who teased James, I'll bet none of them became half the man James has become. Not half.

I admire him. I do. Do you know how good that feels? Do you know how worthwhile that makes my life feel? And I owe that to Jesus, I owe it to him. He gave my son what I couldn't — a purpose . . . a point . . . a friend. I can't tell you how good it feels to admire your own son, to know he is a good man . . . one of the best, really. One of the best!

Part Seven

Order of Service: **"Parenting for Discipleship"**

Monolog: *"The Mother of Jesus"*

Parenting for Discipleship

The Prelude

The Call to Worship

Leader: We gather together this [day/night], knowing that we need to rededicate our lives.

People: We must once again commit ourselves to the work of being Christian disciples.

Leader: We must find in this worship the flame of faith, that which will ignite our discipleship and free us to pick up our crosses and follow Him.

All: Let the spark of His Spirit be with us. Amen

The Opening Hymn   "O Jesus, I Have Promised"

The Litany of Confession

Leader: Forgive us, O Christ, our failure to act.

People: We do know exactly what it means to preach Good News to the poor, to bind the broken-hearted.

Leader: Forgive us, O Christ, our failure to be peacemakers.

People: We do know how to forgive, and the importance of being forgiven. We do know how to admit mistakes, and to accept responsibility when we are wrong.

Leader: Forgive us, O Christ, our failure to show mercy.

People: We do know that you have called us to be passionate in our compassion, and to emphathize with the pain of others, as well as their needs.

Leader: Forgive us, O Christ, our failure to take risks.

People: We do know how safe we choose too often to be, and how seldom we stand up for our beliefs. We do know that too much of our security is materialistic.

All: **Free us, O Christ, to become living sacrifices, a people dedicated to the tasks of discipleship. Amen**

The Assurance of Pardon

The Scripture Lesson   Matthew 5:3-16

The Anthem

The Monolog

A Time for Silent Meditation

The Special Creed

ALL: We believe that discipleship is an art, a craft that requires patience and perseverance. We believe that to be a disciple begins first with a willingness to put someone else's needs before one's own. We believe that true acts of discipleship are fostered by surrender to the will of Jesus Christ.

We beleive that to be a disciple is the toughest task of life, but yields the greatest satisfaction and inner peace. In choosing to follow Christ, we accept our responsibility to build the Kingdom, a territory of truth, and a land layered in love. Though it is easy to admire Christ, it is never easy to follow him. To follow Christ is a great risk, for often we must sacrifice the opinion of the world.

We believe that to become the disciple Christ calls us to become necessitates that we be people committed to justice and equality, peace and peacemaking, mercy and compassion.

The Offering

The Doxology

The Prayer of Dedication

The Lord's Prayer

The Closing Hymn   "The King of Love My Shepherd Is"

The Charge

Leader: Go in peace, serve the Lord.
All: **He has chosen us! Let us follow! Let us be His friends and His disciples! Let us be His church!**

The Benediction

The Postlude

Monolog

The Mother of Jesus

Above all else, let the humanness, the woman, the mother dominate this characterization. Do not fall into playing Mary as a "saint-caricature," or with the dimension of a statue. Give Mary her full scope of human feelings, and the full depth of a mother who has lost a son.

Certainly there have been times . . . times when I have understood . . . understood everything. Yes, there have been times when I somehow knew in my heart exactly why . . . why I was to give birth to God's son, as well as my own; why I would have to watch him leave the comfort and contentment of our home, only to see him persecuted and reviled; why I would watch the world devour my son . . . just eat him up alive.

Yes, there have been times of clarity. But they have been few. You think of me as not merely a woman of faith, but a woman of perfect faith.

I am not. There is no such thing.

I am human. My faith is human . . . flawed . . . imperfect. Yes, there have been days where my faith filled me to the point of bursting, days on the mountaintop where I could see everything in every direction . . . north, south, east, west, inside, outside. At times my faith was so swollen I literally ached with love, the love God gave me, the love God gave me to give. I did have moments of perfect God-created faith. Yes, there have been times when God seemingly pumped me full of the Truth, the Truth that my son was to be the Son of God, the Son of Man . . . the Truth that my son would

save the world . . . the Truth that my son would destroy sin
. . . the Truth that my son would be destroyed by sin. Yes,
indeed, I have been so close to the Truth that I have felt it's
scalding breath. I have been warmed by its heat. I have been
burned by its fire. I have been scorched by its light. I have
been transformed by its miracle.

Still, don't be deceived: there have been valleys of doubt
between those mountain peaks. There have been deserts of
despair that have consumed many days, many nights. There
have been times when I wandered so aimlessly, so hollow
on the inside, so bloated with blind rage that I could not have
seen the eternal eyes of Truth if they stared me straight in
the face.

I am a woman of faith, yes, but I am a *woman,* a human
being, and I have known more than my fair share of terror.
He was my son . . . my flesh . . . my breath. For nine months
he *was* me. He was a part of me, a blessed attachment, an
appendage, a blossoming morsel of my true self. I loved him
as a mother, as only a mother can love — a mother who
will let his tears flow down my cheeks; a mother whose
stomach twirls every time she witnesses his pain; a mother
whose neck tightens every time she knows he hurts; a mother
whose eyes fill everytime she knows he is no longer mine.

I am a woman of faith, yes, but I am a mother, and as
a mother I have been ripped and torn inside by what has
happened to my son. Do you not think that my nights were
not haunted by wild paralyzing fear each time I heard
another plot to take his life? Do you not think that my days
were not possessed in an anxious anguish in watching him
beat his head against a wall trying to make the world sane?
Do you have any idea what it feels like to see your child ooze
with love, flow with fairness, be a person of such kindness
and gentleness and infinite patience, and yet be mocked and

rejected by his friends and neighbors — *our* friends and *our* neighbors? Do you not know that I have felt such anger with God, such vile loathing, that I have wanted to spit . . . to spit upon the Truth . . . to spit upon the Word of God . . . to spit upon the Revelation of God's Wisdom? That Truth, that Word, that Revelation cost me my son . . . my son . . . *my son!*

I know you . . . I know what you are thinking. I am supposed to be the perfect woman, the perfect lady. And spitting at God? How repulsive an image for the woman of perfect faith! I am a mother. I am a mother. (She says it deliberately the third time.) I . . . am . . . a . . . mother.

I watched my son carry a cross. Thorns were buried in his head. Nails were plunged into his wrists and feet. They spat upon him. They whipped him . . . mocked him . . . pierced his flesh with swords.

And you want me to protect your silly notion of the "perfect lady"? You want me to maintain your "unholy" image of a woman without rage, a woman without revulsion, a woman without doubt?

Do you think it was my son alone who felt forsaken?

Do you think it was my son alone who was crucified?

I am his mother. I died too. I felt each nail like a piece of straw scraping across both of my open eyes. I wore that thorny crown around a head that was already shredded in grief. On that day I lost my heart . . . my soul . . . my spirit. Life drained out of me and seemed to flow like a river of sewage to the sea. On that day I came to know darkness, a darkness so deep, so thick, so oily, that my heart felt like a rotting carcass — brittle . . . beaten . . . stinking . . . shriveled . . . decaying. I was plunged into a darkness that converted my heart into a corpse. On that day the dawn died. The sun seemed to be swallowed whole by a ravenous horizon.

66

I hope I have not offended you, or your image of me.
I just simply wanted you to know me as more, as more than
a vision of perfection. I want you to know me as a woman,
as a human being, and as a mother. I need you to know me
as a mother, because then you can accept that your faith
can risk the rage, the doubt, the despair . . . (She gives a
quiet laugh.) . . . even the spitting. You still hate that image, don't you? The spitting mother. Your hate of that image could never compare to the hate I felt in watching my
son crucified. It just won't compare. If you need to, keep your
image, but I will keep my faith that can embrace my rage,
a faith that will tolerate my hate.

Yes, yes, yes, I know. The dawn did not die, really. I knew
you were wondering. The sun has risen again. My son has
risen as well. When my heart felt broken forever, my heart
and mind was seized by a most powerful and poignant por-
trait. I knew that God wept with me. I knew that God wailed
with me. I knew that God spat with me. we both had lost
our son. And then I knew I was not alone. And then I knew
that dawn would return.

My son became more alive for me after that darkest day
than when he was at my side, or even tucked in under my
breast. He filled my days and my nights with a magnificent
peace, a magnificent purpose, a fulness of meaning. I knew
then that all he had lived for was not only true, it was eternal, and that he had won. His love would never end. His hope
would never be extinguished. His Kingdom would become.

From the depths of the Cross to the pinnacle heights of
the Resurrection, that is the flow, the gentle rocking movement of our faith, yours and mine. Like you, I have found
that flow to be at times a hurricane of chaotic confusion,
and at other times the serene slow movement of clarity and
abundant faith. As his mother, I proclaim to you that he

lives, and that he will weep with you, wail with you, spit with you, (laughing) . . . and he will laugh, rejoice, celebrate with you.

He is no longer mine. He is yours. I ask of you only one thing. Love him like a mother. Know him like a mother. Believe in him like a mother.

He is no longer mine. He is yours. Take care of him for me, won't you? I trust you. I really do. Whether you are I know you know, how to be a good mother to him. I expect you to love him as I did . . . my son . . . your Son.

I have finally let him go. I have finally said good-bye. I have finally found the faith to know that he must be yours now . . . all of him . . . for all time.

God bless you. I do . . . trust . . . you.

About the Author

William R. Grimbol is Director of the Shelter Island (New York) Community Youth Program. His wife, Christine, is pastor of the Sag Harbor Presbyterian Church. He has conducted over thirty retreats, seminars and workshops for parents and for youth. He is the chairperson of Youth Ministry Advocates for the Presbytery of Long Island and serves as consultant to the Greenport, New York alternative educational program.

A graduate of St. Olaf College and Princeton Theological Seminary, he is the author of six publications, including the present volume.

The Grimbols are the parents of one son.

www.ingramcontent.com/pod-product-compliance
Lightning Source LLC
Chambersburg PA
CBHW071957070426
42453CB00008BA/986